THE PRACTICAL WAY TO SIMPLIFY YOUR COMPLICATED LIFE

SIMPLY ORGANIZED!

CONNIE COX AND CRIS EVATT

Illustrations by Kathryn Schmidt

W9-CBE-312

B

BERKLEY BOOKS, NEW YORK

SIMPLY ORGANIZED!

A Berkley Book / published by arrangement with
G. P. Putnam's Sons

PRINTING HISTORY
Perigee Books edition published 1988
Berkley edition / June 1991

ISBN: 0-425-10388-6

A BERKLEY BOOK ® TM 757,375
Berkley Books are published by The Berkley Publishing Group,
200 Madison Avenue, New York, New York 10016.
The name "BERKLEY" and the "B" logo
are trademarks belonging to Berkley Publishing Corporation.

PRINTED IN THE UNITED STATES OF AMERICA

10 9 8 7 6 5 4 3

Do you need a helping hand in organizing your home—and your life?

Turn to
Simply Organized!,
the unique motivational approach to living a simpler, less stressful, and more rewarding life.

- Curb your "pack-rat" tendencies
- Discover how a cluttered home breeds *more* clutter!
- Let go of the "power of possessions"—and enjoy the freedom of a simplified lifestyle
- Devise systems that make every task more manageable—from opening the mail to grocery shopping
- Enjoy the simple elegance of an uncluttered home
- Discover storage space savers for closets, kitchen and bathroom
- Set up an efficient home office
- Organize your children, from storing toys and games to returning library books on time
- Delegate household responsibilities to *every* family member
- Create time for yourself without guilt—and learn the value of not doing anything at all!
- Reflect on the simple approach to a complicated world—and see how it changes your ability to cope with everyday stress

Thank you to Theo Gund who researched simplifying and organizing for years and shared many of the quotes she collected. Most of all, we appreciate her ongoing commitment to the idea that simplifying our lives is essential and must be communicated to the world. Thanks also to Candice Fuhrman for contributing her publishing expertise, Kathryn Schmidt for the wonderful illustrations, and to our literary agent, Carol Mann, for her persistence and patience. And thanks to our editor, Adrienne Ingrum, for her excellent editing and, most of all, for her faith in this book.

And of course, thanks to our husbands and families. Cris's husband, Dave, understands simplifying so well that they lived on a 43-foot sailboat for a year and a half sailing to the South Seas. Connie and her husband, Jon, lead a more complicated life juggling three children, Jon's law practice, and Connie's business and volunteer activities. Simplifying for them is a constant challenge and it takes the commitment of everyone in the family.

And thanks to you the reader for giving us any feedback that may help us to communicate this message to others.

This book is dedicated to our
friend and mentor, Theo Gund,
who continues to impress us with
the joys of living simply.

Contents

Introduction

It's time to simplify! Getting through the day has become far too complex. Contemporary women as workers, wives and mothers are overextended, stressed out and frantic. They are, voluntarily or involuntarily, juggling too many activities, possessions and responsibilities. Women are so busy rescuing others that they have no time to rescue themselves. No wonder they are being called "Superwomen."

As organization experts, we have solutions for the Superwoman syndrome. In this book are principles, tips and quotes that will teach you how to live more simply, how to organize and how to delegate. "Simplify, organize and delegate" are three very powerful words symbolizing a way to a more comfortable and rewarding life.

We wrote this book after spending many years thinking about, practicing and teaching the ideas we advocate. Connie is an attorney who was juggling three children, husband and career when she began looking for an easier way. What she learned inspired her to begin teaching others through her *Home Management Systems* seminars. Her newsletter, *Systems UPDATE*, reaches more than 2,000 women in the western United States.

Cris is an author, lecturer and consultant on organizing and home management. Her books, *How to Organize Your Closet and Your Life* and *How to Pack Your Suitcase...and Other Travel Tips*, have helped thousands of women (and men) get organized.

We believe that successful living is a journey toward simplicity and a triumph over confusion. In this book, we'd like to take you on that journey.

—Cris Evatt and Connie Cox

to do today
- [ ] office meeting
- [ ] club meeting
- [ ] school
- [ ] doctor
- [ ] groceries
- [ ] drugstore
- [ ] shoe repair
- [ ] present
- [ ] call Sally
- [ ] air the room
- [ ] car repair

1. Life Is Complicated

I have only one life and it is short enough. Why waste it on things I don't want most?

—Louis Brandeis

We're not here for a long time. We're here for a good time. But how can we have a good time if life is so complicated by maintenance? Woman's work—repetitive, noncreative, mundane—is never done, whether she works inside or outside the home, or more likely these days, in both places.

THE WORKING WOMAN

Five days a week, she arises at dawn, exercises, grooms, eats her Pritikin breakfast, then dashes off to work. She serves The Company all day, then returns home exhausted. She manages to steam dinner, have a meaningful conversation with a few friends, then fall listlessly into bed to watch the ten o'clock news and drop off to sleep. Her weekends are spent catching up—on the wash, haircuts, socializing and shopping. She's a busy woman whether single or attached.

THE FULL-TIME HOMEMAKER

She is up before the children, who must be brushed, dressed, and fed for school. After they've gone, she tidies up the house, then readies herself for myriad errands and volunteer activities. If she's got little ones at home, she monitors their every move like a general or carts them to a sitter—not just any sitter, but a reliable, loving surrogate. She is on the move until the troops are bedded.

THE WORKING MOTHER

She is twice as busy as the other women. She is up at dawn getting herself and her children ready to meet the challenges of the day. She carts the kids to a sitter or to school before she commutes to work. She may feel guilty for leaving the kids and she misses them too. She works hard all day, then returns home to try to meet the endless needs of her children. She is torn between wanting to spend quality time with the kids, needing to cook dinner and clean up, having to do household chores, hoping to have a few moments to spend with her husband and needing to take care of herself after a long day. If she is single, she has one less person to nurture and a lot less income.

Most women today are superwomen—super busy, with little time for themselves. And every woman is a home manager. Have you ever thought about the job of home manager? Connie Cox has, and she has defined the job in its entirety. She tells her seminar students, "Home management tasks are *circular* in nature. Life altering accomplishments are *linear*. Both are essential for a well-balanced life. If either part of life dominates, frustration occurs." She says that a woman who is "always going, creating and becoming" will not succeed if maintenance is neglected. Her life will run amok because disorganization will make her ineffective. On the other hand, "a life dedicated to maintenance" is not very stimulating. Eventually repetition and the lack of creativity are intolerable.

Most women spend too much time on maintenance and become burned out. Connie's Home Manager Job Description, which follows, lists repetitive, noncreative, mundane chores that can never be finished. As you are washing the clothes, someone is out there making others dirty. As soon as all the bills are paid, a new one arrives in the mail. When the dishes are washed, more are dirtied. The dinner is cooked and gone in fifteen minutes. The floor is mopped and crackers are crumbled. The lawn is watered and is dry again in a matter of hours. The kids' hair gets cut and it grows back. Women's work is unending.

Anne Morrow Lindbergh, in her book *Gift from the Sea* (New York: Vintage, 1978), writes eloquently about the problem of being a woman. "For to be a woman is to have interests and duties, raying out in all directions from the central mother core, like spokes from the hub of a wheel. The pattern of our lives is essentially circular. We must be open to all points of the compass: husband, children, friends, home, community; stretched out, exposed, sensitive like a spider's web to each breeze that blows, to each call that comes. How difficult for us, then, to achieve a balance in the midst of these contradictory tensions, and yet how necessary."

HOME MANAGER JOB DESCRIPTION

Executive Director. General director of home in charge of master calendar, hiring and firing all personnel, and maintaining a high level of spirit and productivity within the home.

Accountant/Bookkeeper. Devises budgets, pays bills and balances accounts. Prepares income tax information.

Secretary. Makes appointments (doctor, dentist, hair, etc.) for all members of the family, receives all phone calls, handles correspondence including thank-you's, special-occasion cards and general business and personal correspondence.

Central Files Clerk. Responsible for setting up and maintaining files pertaining to all aspects of the household including financial, educational, social and cultural interests.

Researcher; Safekeeper of Documents. Responsible for providing information on and maintaining documents on the following:

Insurance. Automobile, homeowners, health and life.

Estate Plan. Has will drawn up and keeps it current.

Investments. Money market, real estate, stocks, bonds, etc.

Bank Accounts. Checking and savings.

Safe Deposit Box. Safekeeping for original and irreplaceable documents, with accurate account of contents.

Credit Cards. Keeps accurate record of credit cards, including numbers and where to call in event of theft or loss.

Historian. Responsible for preserving the meaningful moments of the family's life in the form of photos and mementos. Maintains camera equipment, takes photos, has photos developed, sorts photos and places them in an album to be kept for posterity. Mementos are maintained and displayed as well.

Manager of Food Services. Plans menus, purchases food, cooks, serves, and cleans up after two to three meals a day, 365 days a year except when meals are eaten out.

Caterer. Plans, shops for, prepares, and serves meals for entertaining.

Purchasing Agent. Responsible for purchasing food, clothing, toiletries, paper products, furnishings and gifts for entire family.

Director of Educational Services. Responsible for the children's schooling, sports, dancing lessons, music lessons, spiritual enrichment programs, and for educational resources in the home.

Travel Agent. Researches, schedules and plans travel for family.

Laundress. Washes, folds and irons clothes, bedding and towels.

Seamstress. Mends and maintains clothes and other fabrics.

Physical Plant Maintenance Person. Responsible for the following:

Daily Cleaning. General pickup; makes beds, etc.

Trash Disposal. Empties kitchen, bedroom, bathroom and office trash as needed. Prepares trash for weekly pickup.

Weekly Cleaning. Thorough cleaning of house; changes beds, washes floors, vacuums, cleans baths, etc.

Periodic Maintenance. Cleans windows, carpets and upholstery.

Houseplant Maintenance. Purchases, repots, waters, clips and feeds houseplants.

Organization. Cleans out and organizes closets, cupboards, drawers, garage and basement. Discards unwanted or out-of-date items.

Repairs. Has all appliances, electronic devices, etc., repaired. Keeps list of potential repair people and a file with all warranties.

Interior Designer and Architect. Plans and designs interior spaces of home, including furniture, window coverings, floor coverings; responsible for all decoration or remodeling.

Gardener. Mows, waters, weeds, and trims lawn, flowers and shrubs.

Landscape Designer. Designs all plantings and outdoor seating in yard.

Animal Shelter Supervisor. Responsible for providing food, water, shelter, exercise and care for pets on a daily basis. Responsible for obtaining licenses and vaccinations. Provides for baby-sitting when primary caretakers are away.

Automobile Maintenance Supervisor.

Automobile Repair. Responsible for repair in the event of breakdown of any of auto's vital functions.

Automobile Semi-Annual Maintenance. Responsible for oil changes, lubrication and other ordinary maintenance as required. Also responsible for having tires changed or rotated as required by wear or change of weather.

Gas, oil and water checks. General maintenance.

Automobile Grooming. Washing and waxing exterior and maintaining interior.

Giver. Responsible for planning, purchasing, wrapping and sending gifts and cards for family, to relatives, friends, teachers, on such occasions as birthdays, Christmas, Father's Day, Mother's Day, Valentine's Day, and Chanukah.

Gopher. Go for repairs (shoes, appliances, etc.), cleaning and other errands...

Chauffeur. Serves on car pools and takes children to school, sports, lessons and friends' houses.

Baby-sitter/Day Care Worker. Responsible for the purely physical maintenance of children, including providing for safety.

Whether you're single or married, have or don't have kids, your job is complicated. This job description probably doesn't even include some of the tasks you perform in maintaining your home. But your job managing a home doesn't have to be so complicated, just because life is complicated. The next chapter will show you why this is so and give you the information you need to get simply organized.

Life Is Complicated

2. Simplify, Organize, Delegate

If you are wise, you will dread a prosperity which only loads you with more.

—Ralph Waldo Emerson

"You've come a long way, baby!" Never before have women had the opportunity to do so much, have so much and be so much. The Women's Movement has given us possibilities our mothers never dreamed about. The opportunity for personal growth is staggering. So is the opportunity to become overextended and emotionally drained. Erica Jong says, "One of the hard-won prizes of the Women's Movement is the right to become terminally exhausted."

In spite of our many new opportunities, women have clung tenaciously to old responsibilities. They have added the new and have not subtracted the old. "Jobs are still structured for men whose wives take care of the details of life, and homes are still structured for women whose only responsibility is running their family," claims Betty Friedan.

So what can the average woman do about her overextended lifestyle? What is Superwoman's salvation? We have come up with some answers—by no means all of the answers—that will put women on a more comfortable track. Our three answers, or Superwomania Solutions, will uncomplicate home management and give you more time for yourself.

SIMPLIFY!

Let go, let go, let go! Less is best, so *do less, have less,* and *be less* when possible. You will have to be the judge of what to give up and what to keep. Just know that *activities, material things* and *relationships* are time and energy consumers. They eat up your life, bite by bite. Make room for doing what you love, having things you treasure and being with the people who mean the most to you. The superfluous can get you down, while essentials will lift you up. Go for quality, not quantity. In chapters 3, 4 and 5, we will discuss your stuff and how to get rid of things you no longer use and love. Apply the simplicity principle to all areas of your life.

ORGANIZE!

Once you have pared down your *doing, having* and *being,* organize what's left. And, hopefully, it won't be much! In chapters 6 through 12 we will present organizing basics. We have discovered many little tricks for creating simple systems that make mundane tasks a breeze. We will also show you how to streamline your home, a must for busy working women and moms who volunteer.

DELEGATE!

Delegating is an art, and you can do it! We have found that it is much easier to delegate a task that has been simplified and organized. Have you ever tried to get someone to work amidst piles of clutter? They don't do too well, do they? In chapters 13 through 15 we explain the nitty-gritty of delegating.

It's hard for women to delegate because often we are instinctively other-directed and reactive. It's easier for women to be there for everyone but themselves. Unfortunately, when you give too much and receive little, resentment brews. If you don't want to become bitchy, learn to delegate. There is an ancient Jewish proverb, "God could not be everywhere. Therefore He made mothers." Relax! Teach others to be more responsible by letting them experience the consequences of their actions.

We were going to make up a bumper sticker that said, "Delegators Do It Less." But we reconsidered.

THE JOYS OF DOING NOTHING

Our friend Theo is a big fan of doing nothing. Her favorite nonactivities are walking, staring into space and "sofa surfing"—just sitting in solitude while birds chirp outside her window. She is firmly against a rush-rush lifestyle, and she espouses "doing half as much in twice the time."

Theo feels that it is while doing nothing that her intuitive self comes out. It is out of boredom that her creative side emerges. She cherishes every minute of doing nothing she can muster in her busy day. She is a firm believer in the dictum: "Don't just do something, sit there!" We agree with Theo. Besides creating time to do things you love to do, include some time for doing nothing, for emptying the contents of your mind.

D.H. Lawrence cherished times when his mind was empty. He once said, "At present I am blank, and I admit it. So I am just going to go on being blank 'til something nudges me from within and makes me know that I am not blank any longer."

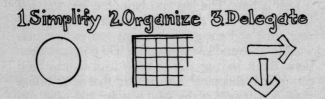

Three Solutions

3. Power of Possessions

Riches prick us with a thousand troubles in getting them, as many cares in preserving them, and yet more anxiety in spending them, and with grief in losing them.

—Saint Francis

Less is best. The less you have, the less you will have to take care of. Really! Material goods gobble your time and energy, so we urge you to have *only* what you use and love in your life. Do not make decisions about buying and keeping stuff lightly. Stop compulsive shopping! Also realize that your things make a statement about who you are and what you value. Do you value quality or quantity? Most of the people we know are slaves to their possessions and don't know it. Here are some facts to ponder:

Possessions clutter. Possessions weigh you down emotionally, cluttering your mind. Casually placed possessions clutter tabletops, closets, counters and garages. Putting stuff away can take all day.

Possessions cost more than the original price. You spend additional money storing, repairing, protecting and cleaning goods. And it takes *time* to cater to them, and lost time is worth money.

Possessions need cleaning. Do you enjoy washing, · dusting, polishing, soaking, scouring and scraping? Even minimal cleaning is time consuming.

Possessions create errands. How many miles a year do you drive to buy, repair and clean your things? How many hours do you spend waiting in store lines and looking for parking? Shopping centers thrive on consumerism.

Possessions are worrisome. Fretting about breakage, loss, theft, fire, repairs and insurance premiums clutters our minds. Every item let go of is one less worry.

Possessions need organizing. Things need to be alphabetized, color coded, sorted and grouped, for sanity's sake. Woe to people who do not know how to organize their things.

Possessions get lost. The less you have, the less you have to lose.

Possessions depreciate. Things that spot, rust, crumble, dent, fray and come unglued lose value. Invest in yourself, not in things.

Possessions are climbed over, hidden, apologized for and argued over. How much more do you need to know?

Possessions encourage greed. Materialistic people tend to compete with their neighbors, brag, hoard and constantly desire more. They are seldom satisfied with what they've got.

As a rule, a man's a fool,
When it's hot, he wants it cool,
And when it's cool, he wants it hot,
Always wanting what is not!

—Anonymous

The price tag at the store is not the true price of possessions. The true price is the original cost plus blood, sweat and tears. The bottom line: Ownership is a prime cause of *stress*.

Working hard to maintain an overmaterialized life-style puts stress on your relationships, your sex life and your finances. It is a cause of divorce, bankruptcy, job dissatisfaction, and declining mental and physical health. Do not become intoxicated or infatuated by, or addicted to possessions. They have the power to own more of you than you own of them.

Bertrand Russell said, "It is the preoccupation with possession more than anything else, that prevents man from living freely and nobly."

Power of Possessions

4. Pack-Rat Factor

That poverty is no disaster is understood by everyone who has not yet succumbed to the madness of greed and luxury which turns everything topsy-turvy. How little a man requires to maintain himself! And how can a man who has any merit at all fail to have that little?

—Seneca

How many times have you heard people say, "If only I could get rid of more things." It's tough throwing things away, and it's painful living with so much stuff. Why are we so weak when it comes to discarding? Why does it take so much courage to let go of unwanted items?

Below is a list of rationalizations that keep people trapped by superfluous possessions. These excuses keep people from being free of clutter, from leading simpler, more carefree lives.

PACK-RAT RATIONALIZATIONS

"If I get rid of things, I'm throwing money away."

You lose more money keeping unused and unloved things around. They occupy expensive space and valuable time. And the cost of space in your home can exceed one hundred dollars per square foot!

"My things remind me of the past."

Relics from the past are attempts to keep it alive. Your present life, with its real people and potent sensations, is more alive. There's a realistic limit on what to keep for memory's sake. In the book *Letting Go: Uncomplicating Your Life*, the author, Ramona A. Adams, observed, "Life is not static: it is dynamic. To live means to outlive. To grow is to outgrow and to let go. Ideas, behaviors, values, friends, and other facets of our lives that were useful at one stage may very well become a burden at another."

"I may use it in the future."

For every one hundred things you think you will use, you may use one. You keep ninety nine to have one that may someday be useful. Why not buy the one again? It's cheaper in the long run.

"Everyone has one, so it must be important."

The new status symbol is to fill your life with things you love—not with what others have. Develop your own personal style for people to admire.

"But it was a gift."

Gifts are symbols of love. Keep the love and let go of the symbols.

"I'll keep it until I find someone to give it to."

Put it in a Goodwill box, where it will go to someone who truly needs it. Don't spend your valuable time— the only truly precious and irreplaceable commodity in your life—looking for a suitable home for it.

"I identify with my things."

Possessions can become psychological appendages of one's personality. Identify with things that truly define you and let the rest go. Connie says, "You are defined by all that you have, including the clutter you can't part with."

"Ugh! It was a mistake."

If you bought it and made a mistake, keeping it around for a long time won't make it any less of a mistake. Either love it, use it, or get rid of it. It's O.K. to make mistakes.

"I don't have time to sort through my things."

Start by getting rid of just one item. Remember, a journey of a thousand miles begins with a single step.

DON'T SLEEP ON THE PORCH

If you would like to simplify your life and have more free time, remember this rule: "Whenever you buy something new, get rid of something unwanted." The number of items that flow into your home should equal the number of items that flow out. There must be a balance of old and new. If you do not follow this rule, you may find yourself seeking a larger home, renting storage space or sleeping on the porch!

Pack-Rat Factor

5. Simply Simplify!

In order to seek one's own direction, one must simplify the mechanics of ordinary, everyday life.

—Plato

Remember the "good old days" when you could load all of your belongings into the back of a VW bug? When you could spend weekends staying up late, sleeping in and sunning all day because you had no lawn to mow, no contractor to meet and no taxes to prepare. What happened? Is your life better now? Are you having more fun with more, more, more?

How do you simplify a complicated lifestyle? Cris Evatt created a three-step procedure for simplifying all aspects of life which she presents in seminars and in her book, *How to Organize Your Closet and Your Life* (New York: Ballantine, 1981). She urges people to begin untangling their lives by weeding out *things*—unwanted and unneeded possessions—in one small area, such as a drawer, glove compartment, counter top or closet. Then, after successfully pruning, she shows you how to organize what's left. First simplify, then organize. Always in that order!

THE MECHANICS OF SIMPLIFYING

Step 1. Sort your things into three piles.

First, choose an area to simplify. Then sort your things into three piles. Take the items out one by one. Hold each item up and ask yourself, "How do I feel about this? Do I love and use it? Am I ambivalent about it? Do I want to discard it?" Take your time with this step.

- **Love and use pile.** Put the things you feel good about and use often in this pile.

- **Ambivalence pile.** Ambivalence means to be attracted to something and repulsed by it at the same time. You seldom use these items because you don't feel good about them, but you hang onto them because of pack-rat rationalizations.

- **Discard pile.** Put the things you never use and *are* willing to get rid of in this pile.

After you have removed everything from the area, clean it thoroughly. Notice how good it feels to see the scrubbed bottom of a drawer, a closet floor or counter-top that had been obfuscated with clutter.

Tip: Signs reading I Love It, I Don't Know, and Out are especially handy when you help children sort their things. And the sorting process encourages children to become uncluttered adults!

Step 2. Remove the discard pile.

There are two types of discarded items: recyclables and throwaways. Put the *throwaways* in a trash basket or rent a dumpster if you have tons of junk.

Recyclables—to be given to Goodwill, the Salvation Army or a thrift store—can be kept in a recycle bin in the garage. Stash things in it every chance you get and then make one giant run to the recycling center. Don't drive from place to place to bestow your beloved castoffs. If you must spread the wealth, choose one place this season and next season, choose another.

Step 3. Create an Ambivalence Center.

Getting the items you're ambivalent about out of your living area—by creating a storage center for them—lets you experience the freedom of living only with the things you love and use. It also lets you practice living without certain items before you make that irreversible decision to give or throw them away.

Imagine a corner of your garage with stacked and labeled cardboard storage chests, which you can buy for about four dollars in stationery and variety stores. Each contains possessions from your closets, drawers, cupboards and the rest of the house that were not being used, but which you aren't ready to get rid of yet. The boxes in the garage give your things a transition zone.

In clothes closets, hang garments from your ambivalence pile at one end, away from the clothes you love to wear. Force yourself to wear these items as soon as possible. If they turn out to be things you love and wear, put them back in with your favorite clothing. If not, recycle them immediately.

Sort through the lidded, labeled boxes in the ambivalence center at least every six months, and get rid of as much as possible. Keeping up with materialism takes vigilance, and the rewards are worth the effort.

GETTING ORGANIZED

Finally, it's time to deal with the things in the love-and-use pile. These are the things that are important to you *now*. Next week or month, they may be meaningless, but today, they are meaningful. Love-and-use items are enjoyed more when they are organized. Develop a systematic way of putting these possessions away, and your focus will be on the possessions, not on the maintenance of them. In the next chapter, we will describe systems.

6. Let's Get Organized!

Organization has nothing to do with duty, morals or virtue. Organization is just the starting point, not the end. It frees you from the frustration and confusion of wasting time. What you do with your time is strictly personal. You may want to use the hours to daydream in the sandbox with your baby, go on movie binges, or write long letters to Ralph Nader. The time will be there for you to do it.

—Theo Gund

To organize, revise any inefficient systems. A system is basically a habit, the way you do a task repeatedly. The routines you use to grocery shop, do the laundry and pay the bills are all systems. So you are not going to create anything new; you are merely going to revise your old ways and change random complex systems into planned simple systems.

There is a big difference between the two kinds of systems. A simple system requires forethought and planning. Once it is set up, it saves you hours of time. A complex system is the result of doing something randomly.

RANDOM COMPLEX SYSTEMS

- Fix it before you wear it.

- Exercise when you feel guilty.

- Clean the house before company comes.

- Pile of shoes on the closet floor.

- Eat now, diet later.

- Water the lawn when it's brown.

How many random systems do you have? Did you identify with the ones above? Or did you find them examples of extreme negligence?

PLANNED SIMPLE SYSTEMS

A systematic approach to life allows it to run smoothly, whereas a random approach creates chaos. But how do you systematize, and what can be cranked out by a system? How can crusty old habits be turned into clever, creative maneuvers? All are questions worth asking if you want more private time—time to write that novel, plant a vegetable garden, hike in the Himalayas or just do nothing. First, let's define successful, productive systems by looking at the four components of systems.

Name.

Give your system an official name. Think, "I'm going to use the laundry system." Don't think, "I'm going to do the laundry." Giving your routine a name upgrades it.

Setup.

Your systems need a location, tools and supplies, and organizers. Where will you store the tools and supplies you will need—in a cupboard, in the filing cabinet, in the car? Will you use bins, hooks, files or dividers? (On Page 43, we elaborate on setups.)

Procedure.

How do people fit into the system? In what order are the steps to be done?

Frequency.

How often will you use your system? Daily, weekly, monthly? Or is it a "spur-of-the-moment" routine?

EXAMPLES OF PLANNED
SIMPLE SYSTEMS

Name: Bill-Paying System

Setup:

In desk—Stamps, envelopes, return-address labels, checkbook, calculator and pile of bills.

Procedure:

1. When bill arrives in mail: open bill, discard ads, put bill in mailing envelope, stamp, affix address label and put due date on outside.

2. At bill-paying time, write check.

3. Enter amount into ledger.

4. Place bill back in envelope.

5. File receipts.

6. Mail.

Frequency:

Pay bills between first and fifth of the month.

Name: Laundry System

Setup:

- In the laundry room—Rack with six large white wire baskets.

- Baskets labeled Darks, Lights, Linens, Deliates, Dry Cleaning, and Mending.

- One box of soap, bleach and a bottle of spot-remover in the cupboard. (Duplicates are in a central storage area.)

- Wall-mounted ironing board and iron.

Procedure:

1. Family members put their clothes into proper baskets.

2. Mom washes and dries clothes.

3. Mom puts laundered clothes on beds of family members.

4. Each person folds and puts away own clothes.

Frequency:

Monday and Thursday—clothes will be laundered.

Wednesday—linens laundered.

Weekends—no laundry will be done.

Before bedtime—clean clothes to be put away; dirty clothes to be in proper baskets.

Name: Gift Wrap System

Setup:

In closet—Rolls of gift wrap in a tall round plastic wastebasket.

Mini laundry basket, containing scissors, tape, ribbon and greeting cards.

System is portable and available to all family members.

Procedure:

1. Take setup to any flat surface to do wrapping.

2. Return setup to closet immediately after use.

Frequency:

Any time you want to give a gift!

There are so many systems to create. We do not want to describe dozens of systems in this book, because systems are individual creations. Maybe you don't like white wire baskets in your laundry room. Maybe you would prefer a series of red plastic baskets on flowered shelves. Think of fabulous systems to suit your lifestyle. Think of a grocery-shopping system, tape-cassette system, a library system, a watering-the-yard system and many more. Have fun putting your mundane tasks in order. Take charge!

MORE ABOUT SETUPS!

If your setups aren't well thought out, your planned simple systems will fall apart. They will become messy and not much better than random complex systems. We have discovered five rules that, if followed conscientiously, will help you organize spaces.

Rule 1. Group like things together.

Put like items together. All kinds of tape, regardless of shape or size, can be stored together. Gardening items can be put together, not scattered around the garage. Hair-care products can be grouped together. For a four-year-old girl, keep buckets of hair ribbons, barrettes, rubber bands and hairbrush all together. Create categories of like items or items used together.

Rule 2. Everything needs a special place.

Any time you find yourself searching for something, like glasses, keys or scissors, find a wonderfully convenient place and keep it there. Remember, no place is convenient if it is a lot of trouble to use. Only simple systems are maintained on an ongoing basis. You don't have to be compulsively neat; you just want to create a sensible space for everything so that when you do clean up, there is a handy place to put things.

There are "general locations"—closets, cupboards, drawers, shelves and counters—for your things; then there are "specific locations"—exact spots within a general location. Organizers separate items and groups of like items from each other and hold them in place.

43

Keep things close to where you will be using them. The best locations are always the handiest. Put the ironing board near the iron, the sewing supplies near the sewing machine and the *TV Guide* near the television. You will save time by not having to walk an extra hundred miles each year.

Rule 3. Buy or make organizers.

Organizers hold systems together. Bins, boxes, jars, hooks, racks, dividers, lazy Susans, labels, files and containers separate things from each other in that "special place" you put them in. Without separators, items will heap on top of one another and create that amorphous mass we fondly refer to as "clutter."

Spend time researching organizers. Check the organizing products in hardware and variety stores. Look for stores that devote their entire inventory to organizers. Buy colorful organizers, but not so multicolored to make you feel cluttered when you look at them. If the colors please you, you will be more apt to keep order. The organizers should be durable, too. You don't want your systems to fall apart along with the organizers. Below are questions to ask yourself when shopping for the perfect organizers:

■ Is it stackable?

■ Can it be used for several purposes?

■ Where will I put it?

■ Is it dishwasher-proof?

- If I spend more, will I get a more durable, functional product?

- How do the colors coordinate?

- Do I really need it, or is it just cute?

Store things in see-through containers unless you will be looking down on items, as in a drawer—then it doesn't matter. If you want to find something easily, put it in a clear plastic container or a wire container with an open weave.

Rule 4. Store few items in each storage area.

Do not cram things into drawers, cupboards and closets. It is hard to be neat when there is too much stuff being stored. This goes back to the simplicity rule: The less you have, the less you will have to care for. Remove from *current* storage anything you don't use at least once a month. Shed these items or put them out of sight in an ambivalence center in your garage or on a high shelf.

Rule 5. Line up and stack things with care.

If you simplify a cupboard, drawer, closet or counter, then keeping things lined up and stacked neatly is feasible. If you have just the number of glasses you and your family use on a lower shelf and glasses for guests on a higher shelf, it will be easy to keep them straight. If you have few linens, they will stay stacked neatly. Take pride in your stacks and line ups. There will be times when disarray is the order of the day. Have high standards and fall a little short now and then. Better than having low standards and falling even shorter.

The purpose of this book is not to make meticulous, neurotic neatniks out of its readers. The point is, if you set up simple systems, you will be able to have order without effort—and order feels good!

POINTS TO REMEMBER!

Any time you have done something before that you're doing now and you can project that you will be doing it again, you ought to make a system. And the simpler your basic systems are, the more adaptable they are to the changes you will encounter in your life and in the lives of the others you live with.

Before you make a system, remember to simplify! Get everything that is not important out of your life. It may be clothing, people, forks and knives in your silverware drawer, the extra lawn mower or the mixer. Simplify your life first and then set up some workable systems.

Let's Get Organized

46

7. Streamlined Spaces

...The cart before the horse is neither beautiful nor useful. Before we can adorn our houses with beautiful objects, the walls must be stripped and beautiful housekeeping and beautiful living be laid for a foundation. Now, a taste for the beautiful is cultivated out of doors, where there is no house or housekeeper.

—Henry David Thoreau

Most people cannot live without their stuff. In fact, they must buy or rent a good sized house just to store their stuff. Their house becomes a giant pile of stuff with a cover on it. How much stuff have you collected? Tons, reams, mounds?

Imagine living in a stark room with a carpet, a window and no furnishings. You notice the view. You notice the ceiling and walls. You notice everything about the room: the colors, shadows, proportions and the quality of the carpet. Could you live in an empty room with a view? What would it be like?

In this chapter, we want to take a fresh look at interior spaces and how they are furnished. We want to encourage you—not to live in an empty room—but to live happily with less. We will present tips for creating a simplified ambience, room by room.

MINIMALISM'S AXIOMS

Fewer Tables

■ Do you have big and little tables everywhere — tables that sit against walls, next to sofas and beside beds. Tables complicate life by collecting clutter. How many tables can you live without?

Clear the Counters

■ Cleared counters give a room a sense of order. If your counters are cluttered, think about finding a special place for everything — even if it's a junk drawer!

Fewer Plants

■ Plants take time to water, fertilize, spray, repot, talk to, serenade and love. Simplify by having a few very large plants, not lots of little plants dotted about the house.

■ Tip: Buy just two large permanent plants — a six foot ficus and a luxurious palm tree. Then occasionally buy pots of colorful flowering plants to give a room color for a month or so.

Clear the Windowsills

■ Nothing makes a home look more cluttered than objects perched near windowpanes. Knickknacks, small bottles, perfumes, pills and sprouting plants obstruct views and look messy. Learn to love the fresh, clear look of sunlight as it filters through un-fettered windows.

Bare the Floors

■ Would you rather clean a floor with four tables, six chairs, seven standing plants, two floor lamps, a magazine basket, two speakers and a pair of matching ceramic elephants, or a floor with none of the above? Unencumber your floors.

Unload Shelves and Drawers

■ It is easy to pack shelves and drawers until they can hold no more. Keep space around stored items. Find what you want faster.

Reduce Lamp Inventory

■ Most lamps need tables to sit on, or they perch on the floor, making a room look choppy. Choose track, recessed or pendant lighting where possible.

Book, Magazine and Newspaper Purge

■ How many times have you seen stacks of old magazines and newspapers in people's homes. How did they make you feel? Weed out periodicals a.s.a.p.! Remember, public libraries have fabulous, well-cataloged collections of magazines ready for you to research any subject at any time. Let them do what they are good at and you do what you are good at.

- Most people keep too many books. Why collect them? Over 55,000 new books come out a year, over 1,000 per week. Read books, enjoy them, grow from them, and then pass them on to friends. If you must keep books, judge them by their reference value.

- Some people keep books around as tangible evidence of their intelligence. Unconsciously, they are saying to visitors, "These books contain the subjects I know about. They aren't just books. They are me." The purpose of education is to teach you to continue to learn and adapt throughout life, not to hold on to dated information.

Eliminate Too Many Patterns

- Interior designers know that a room can be filled with too many patterns, prints and colors. One needs open space and background against which to display fine art work or pieces of furniture. Life is the same. Make the backdrop of life well ordered, plain and simple so that the rich experiences of life can come through in technicolor.

Learn to Love Empty Spaces

- Empty spaces are peaceful to look at and live with. Cleared counters and furniture free areas do not demand attention. They leave your mind free to think creative and idle thoughts.

- Have few things and see each one often. A precious vase is enjoyed more when it is surrounded by empty space and does not have to compete with other objects.

SIMPLE ELEGANCE

Simple living can be aesthetically pleasing. Envision uncluttered rooms with all of the amenities for elegant living. Make your home a neutral canvas onto which brighter colors and aggressive textures can be applied at will. Of paramount importance is natural sunlight flooding onto surfaces, making playful shadows throughout the day.

The rooms have a predominantly straight-line geometry that can be broken up by mirrors and a casual placement of a luxuriant plant. A plush oversized sofa and chairs are comfortable and inviting, as comfort is of prime importance. Each room is remembered for one wonderful thing that stands out—an exotic carpet, a priceless lacquered screen, a favorite antique quilt on the wall.

Living simply does not mean living like a miser in austere surroundings. It means enjoying your life more than ever in an easy-care, pleasing, serene environment. A home should be a restful retreat for its members, especially the primary home manager. The less there is to clutter and to manage, the more opportunity there is for enjoyment. Now let's look at each room in the house.

Streamlined Spaces

Living Room

The living room is for comfortable relaxation. It is for recreation, for entertaining favorite friends. Make people and activities the focus of your living room—not small trinkets, worn out paperbacks and lamps that need dusting. A few strong statements best represent you.

Sofas

- Living comfortably is a prime feature of living simply. A well designed, L-shaped sofa makes the most economical use of space.

- A seating group that has more than three or four permanent pieces tends to look overwhelming. Plan a simple configuration. You can always add occasional chairs.

Coffee Tables

- The coffee table is the only table you absolutely need in the living room. Place from one to three items on your coffee table—i.e., a current magazine, a pot of flowers and one object d'art. More than three pieces is the beginning of clutter.

End Tables

- End tables are magnets for dust and clutter. At the sides of a sofa, they make the living room look like a shrine. To simplify, exclude end tables and replace table lamps with overhead lighting or floor lamps. The sofa table behind a couch can be a useful and often hidden addition.

Speakers

- Hang speakers or place them in a wall unit. When they sit on the floor, they attract small ornaments.

Floor Lamps

- Floor lamps are easy to move when vacuuming and don't need a table. They make good reading lamps. Track lighting requires less maintenance than either floor or table lamps. Choose overhead lighting whenever convenient.

A Simply Decorated Living Room

- A simply decorated living room might have an L-shaped sofa, a generous coffee table, track lighting and a floor lamp for reading, a wonderful painting or two, a warm fireplace, and mini blinds which can be opened to reveal a breathtaking view. Add a very large plant to soften a corner of the room.

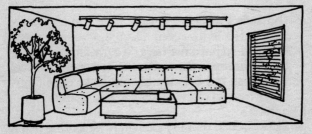

Living Room

Bedroom

The bedroom is for relaxing, sleeping and dressing. The presence of a desk, paperwork and things to do make it a complicated, stressful place.

Dressers Evaluated

- Eliminate bedroom dressers whenever possible. Dressers collect paraphernalia on top, are time consuming to open, and personal belongings can become hidden and forgotten in drawers.

- Built-in shelving in the clothes closet is best. You can put clothing away quicker and find items easier. Lingerie can be put in baskets, bins or built-in drawers.

- Small bedrooms feel more spacious without dressers. Put a large ficus where your dresser used to be.

Beds Made Easy

- To simplify, put a mattress on a platform or drawer base. Eliminate the under-the-bed space that collects dust and belongings, and looks ugly. (You'll never have to clean under the bed again!)

- Platform bed drawers are handy for storing bed linens. You won't have to trek down the hallway for sheets and pillowcases. Also, they are a great place to store heavy woolen sweaters and ski accessories.

Down Comforters

■ Choose a light, cuddly down comforter instead of blankets and a bedspread. Protect it with a pillowcaselike cover that can be tossed in the wash. Bed making becomes a breeze.

Nightstands

■ Keep only current reading material on your nightstand. It is not a library or a bookshelf. Nor is it a filing cabinet for torn-out articles or old magazines. Keep rotating reading material.

■ Nightstands, like dressers, are clutter collectors. To simplify, design a bedside table that is a single shelf-like surface extending from your bed or the wall. Eliminate nightstand drawers, which hold little things—pins and pens, forgotten business cards, letters and souvenir matches.

Decorator Bed Pillows

■ Admittedly, they are cute, but ten of them on your bed? It takes time to set petite pillows aside before you retire, and it takes time to put them back on your bed in the morning. It takes time to clean and repair them, and it took time to pick them out.

Bedroom Windows

■ The simplified bedroom features mini blinds, not fluffy curtains, or drapes that hang to the floor collecting dust. Mini blinds regulate light wonderfully and have a sleek appearance.

- Clear the bedroom windowsills. It's much easier to clean sills without plants, perfumes or knickknacks on them.

Televisions

- If you have a television set in the bedroom, suspend it from a wall with a sturdy bracket or put it in a handsome wall unit. Avoid tiny tables which clutter and collect.

Wall Lamps

- For reading in bed, wall lamps are attractive and efficient; they do not fall over, take up space or add confusion to the bedroom.

Guest Bedrooms

- How often do guests use your guest bedroom? If the answer is less than once a month, turn the bedroom into a home office and become more organized. Or buy a smaller home, which is easier to maintain. Leonardo da Vinci said, "Small rooms or dwellings set the mind in the right path, large ones cause it to go astray."

Bedroom

Closet

Most of us have closets that are stuffed full. And even if the situation isn't that bad, we certainly wouldn't put our closets on a public tour. A philosophy has built up around people's closets. If they are cluttered, then so must be the owner's mind. Put your closet in order and the state of your mind will follow. And the easier it will be to stumble into your closet in the morning to retrieve your clothes, the better your day will go! Conquer cluttered closets.

Tip: Don Johnson is escaping from a mob of adoring fans. He arrives at your door. "Quick! Hide me in your closet!" Would you die of embarrassment? Always keep your closet ready for handsome strangers.

Wire-Hanger Purge

- Replace wire hangers with plastic tubular hangers (except for the wire hangers that hold clothes you're ambivalent about at the back of your closet). Plastic tubular hangers are inexpensive, about thirty cents a piece. Buy a good-quality brand because some are cheaply made and break easily or snag garments.

- Plastic tubular hangers are superior to wire hangers because they don't misshape the shoulders of shirts, light-weight sweaters and T-shirts. They are easy to handle and space garments nicely. They are great for drip-drying clothes because they don't create rust marks. They are colorful and attractive!

- Use only one hanger color. Display the clothes, not the hangers.

- Children's plastic hangers are great for small-sized women's clothes. Pants don't slide back and forth. T-Shirts fit well.

Up with Shoes

- Get shoes off the closet floor (if possible), so they don't get jumbled and dusty. The best place for shoes is lined up on the shelf above the clothes. If you need the space above the shoes, add another shelf. Second best, use a hanging shoe bag or shoe rack on the door.

Laundry Bag for Dry Cleaning

- It is great to keep a laundry bag in the master closet for clothes to go to the dry cleaners. It eliminates piles of clothes waiting to be taken for cleaning.

Boot Trick

- Roll up magazines lengthwise and stuff them into your boots. The boots will stand upright on a closet shelf. If you don't use a boot stuffer of some sort, your boots will be more wrinkled around the ankles.

Towel Racks

- Two to four kitchen or bath towel racks can be hung on the back of your closet door. They are great for scarves and tablecloths. If you buy thick, rounded racks, you can hang pants over them.

Hooks and Nails

■ Ceramic hooks can be hung all over your closet for hats, belts, bags and jewelry. Nails are good for belts that won't fit on the hooks.

Peg-Boards

■ Cover the back of your closet door or a wall in your closet with Peg-Board. Hang belts, hats or jewelry. A great multipurpose idea!

Sleeping Bag Tip

■ Hang sleeping bags, whether down or synthetic filled, over strong plastic hangers. They need to breathe and shouldn't be left rolled up.

Recycling Clothes

■ Have a fabric laundry bag in every person's closet to hold outgrown or tiresome clothes. Every so often, go around and collect the bags and dump them into a central recycling area or the box for the next child.

Stockings

■ Put dirty stockings into a mesh laundry bag with a tie, then toss the bag into the washer with your other clothes. Mesh bags are also good for delicate lingerie.

Wardrobe Freeze

- If too many clothes is your problem, consider allowing yourself only a fixed number of items. Limit yourself to a certain number of skirts, dresses, blazers, etc., and never allow yourself to accumulate more. If you want to update, or if you find a dress you cannot resist, then eliminate something from your wardrobe. Go for quality, not quantity. This has helped many compulsive shoppers.

  Remember what Chanel said: "True elegance consists not in having a closet bursting with clothes, but rather in having a few well chosen numbers in which one feels totally at ease."

Wire Basket System

- A system of wire baskets, shelves and rods lets you create the perfect closet and can take just minutes to assemble. Wire basket drawers pull out effortlessly, even when filled, and keep contents well ventilated. Choose from a wide range of frame and drawer sizes to create your own personalized storage solution. Such systems can also be used in the laundry room, pantry and office.

Sweater Boxes

- Sweaters have a way of sliding when you stack them. You can keep them wrinkle free, dust free and right where you want them in durable, see-through plastic boxes. The boxes are designed for stacking and have close-fitting lids. You'll love them and moths won't.

Hanging Iron and Board

■ You can hang your iron and board right where you want them — out of the way. Look for ironing-board caddies. Several manufacturers make them. Or make your own! Place the duo on the back wall of a walk-in closet or on a wall in your laundry room.

Hobbies vs. Necessities

■ Make things that you don't care much about simple — those things that are not required for hobbies or great interests. For instance, have one lipstick that goes with your skin and hair color; have one or two basic purses. However, if makeup, clothes and accessories are your hobby, then have more so you can enjoy the nuances of mixing and matching. Then set up a terrific system for accessories.

Closet

Kitchen

The kitchen is a workplace. Make working in it simple, straightforward and, therefore, rewarding. Having to move plants, magazines, mail and other personal belongings makes working in the kitchen frustrating. Keep the kitchen visually restful so you can focus on the task at hand. Copy the convenient layout at a cooking-school demonstration. Cooking is the focus, not storage of the family clutter.

Clear Kitchen Counters

- Clean, cleared counters look chic and orderly. If you must have anything on your counters, limit items to those used *daily*. Maybe you use a toaster oven, coffee maker and grinder, and a crock of wooden spoons often enough to merit being on the counters rather than hidden in drawers.

Hanging Pots

- Pots and pans stored in cupboards are hard to retrieve. Hang kitchenware used daily on a high-tech wall grid in your favorite color, or on hooks suspended from a sturdy, metal, overhead rectangular or oval ceiling rack.

Accessible Shelving

- Things stored on deep and inaccessible shelving are hard to retrieve too. Try roll-out shelves, which can be made of wood or purchased in plastic.

- When given a choice, choose drawers over shelving. Everything is visible from the top.

- Open shelves allow you to get what you want in seconds. They are timesavers, even though some people feel that having everything in sight confuses the mind. Use your own judgment.

Identify Work Centers

- Researchers from Cornell University came up with the concept of "work centers" for the kitchen. A work center is where a cook performs specific tasks, e.g., cleaning, chopping, cooking. Each center has a major appliance (i.e., stove, refrigerator, sink), some storage and a work surface. Study your kitchen and create work centers.

- Store items of equipment and food near the center where they will be used. Store pots and pans near the stove, baking goods and utensils near the mixer, and dishes near the sink and dishwasher. Save steps!

- The lunch box center: store all makings for lunches and snacks—juices, bread, nuts, fruit, lunch bags, sandwich bags and straws—in one place. It may mean having another set of plastic bags in another location for another purpose.

The work center concept is common sense, but as Voltaire once said, "Common sense is not so common." Maybe you hadn't thought of it.

Clipping Tips

- Use large clips or a clipboard to hang things in the kitchen, such as paper bags, place mats or even magazines.

The Errand Drawer

- Devote a roomy drawer or basket in the kitchen to errands. Use it to hold shoes to be fixed, books to be returned to the library, pans to be returned to a neighbor, etc.

Herbs and Spices

- Spices and herbs can be stored upright in a kitchen drawer. Put colorful, circular labels on the top of each lid for identification. Spices keep longer in the dark.

- Buy rarely used spices from the bulk jars at a health-food store. Buy only the amount needed.

Glasses Drink Up Space

- Keep only the glasses you use. Calculate how many glasses you need, then subtract that number from the number of glasses you own. Get rid of extras or store them out of the way. Free your cupboard space. Line up your glasses in neat rows according to type. Stacking glasses are great.

Kitchen Extras

- Keep only the utensils you use frequently. Store seldom-used ones in a shoe box on a top shelf for that special dinner.

- Extraneous pots and pans, bowls, casseroles and dishes may be stored up high or in the basement/garage. Keep only items used weekly handy in the kitchen. You'll feel better!

Coupons Are Costly

- Unless you really use coupons, don't collect them. Unused, they are time wasters—they have to be found, clipped, stashed, remembered and redeemed. And often, one buys what one doesn't need because *so much* money is seemingly saved.

Cookbook Collections Grow Unnoticed

- How many cookbooks do you use? How many do you have? Keep treasured books. Let the rest go.

- File favorite, often-used recipes by category in inexpensive photo albums.

- Recipes cut out of magazines and newspapers are rarely used. Sort through yours, and let go of ancient formulas. If you must keep them, put untried recipes in an accordion file by category.

Thin-Within Refrigerators

- Refrigerators can become overloaded with food and condiments that need to be updated or eliminated. Keep current with foodstuffs. Find foods faster in an unstuffed refrigerator.

- Lazy Susans work well on some refrigerator shelves to hold tall bottles and cartons. Twirling bottles are a quick snatch. Bi-level lazy Susans work well for small items like yogurt, mustard and jam.

- Plastic mini laundry baskets can be filled with sandwich makings. Use another basket for kiddie snacks.

- Use only clear, see-through containers.

- Keep the top of the refrigerator free of clutter. A bowl full of junk is not a peaceful sight.

Few Appliances

- Labor-saving devices do not necessarily save labor. Is that shocking? Appliances need to be kept clean, stored after use, repaired if broken, and they have ugly cords. Warranties need to be filed and found. Some appliances are essential, others are not. Know the difference.

- Trash compactors, electric can openers, food processors, hot-dog cookers, juicers, electric knives and popcorn poppers complicate life. Try standing on the trash, opening cans the old way, chopping your carrots and onions, boiling hot dogs, eating the whole orange, cutting the turkey by hand and popping corn in a pot.

Notebook by the Phone

- A household with several busy members has many rosters, club lists, school lists, committee lists and sports schedules. Put these lists in a loose-leaf notebook by the phone for everyone to use. This is also an excellent place to put baby-sitter instructions, grocery lists and menus from take-out food places.

Kitchen

Bathroom

The bathroom sees your sleepy eyes and disheveled morning hair. It awakens you with its warm beating shower and bristling brushes. It readies you to greet the day. Make it simple so you can muddle through it in a fog and still get everything done.

Tidy Vanities

- Clear the vanities! People clutter vanity counters with perfumes, combs, mousse, toothbrushes, plants and seashell art. Keep only soap and hand lotion handy.

Packed Medicine Cabinets

- Medicine-cabinet shelves attract stuff. How many forgotten nail polishes, deodorants, medicines and creams do you have? Sparsely supply your medicine cabinets with only things you use every day, then shine those little glass shelves!

Orderly Bathroom Drawers

- A plastic drawer divider with movable subdividers is a way to keep like items together in a bathroom drawer.

- Plastic silverware trays with rectangular divisions also make drawers neat. Toothbrushes, paste and floss can go in one tray. Hairbrushes, combs and other hair items can go in another.

Washing Shower Curtains

- Put shower curtains in a washing machine with warm, soapy water and three bath towels. Water spots will vanish from the vinyl.

Bathroom Storage Tips

- When you no longer use an item, such as hot rollers, but cannot bear to throw it away, remove from the bathroom and store with other outdated items for the bath. (At least place in a container on a very high shelf.)

- Store bathroom products bought in advance (such as toilet paper and soap) in a central place, not with already opened items.

- If you have not used a cosmetic, toiletry or medicine for six months, place it in the storage container with other items of its kind, or throw away.

- Keep the towels you use on an ongoing basis in the bathroom. The rest can be stored in the linen closet or possibly sent to old-towel heaven. You only need a few old towels for when the kids go to the beach or the pool.

- Bath toys are nicely stored in a wicker basket. Baskets look good, absorb water and let toys air out.

- Keep all travel items, such as a travel hair dryer, pre-packed toiletries kit, and cosmetic bag, in one container (a mini laundry basket) so they are all together and ready to go when you travel.

Six-Month Bathroom Shopping

- Buy a six-month supply of shampoo, deodorant, toothpaste, soap and razors. Store in a central storage area.

- Buy gallon sizes of shampoo, then refill a small-sized bottle.

- Buy cases of toilet paper, and you won't run out for six months.

Bathroom

8. Set Up a Home Office

Running a home is like running a small business. Thousands of dollars go through a household yearly. Mortgage or rent payments must be made. Insurance is researched, purchased and kept track of. Home maintenance and home improvements need to be planned, executed and recorded. Household bills — utilities, telephone, groceries, credit cards, car payments, medical and educational bills — are paid. All of this requires accounting and filing systems. And remember, unless the systems are simple and easily maintained, they won't be, and life will become a series of piles.

In addition, many other household functions resemble the running of a small business. Appointments are made and recorded for doctors, dentists and haircutters. Menus are planned. Grocery lists are made. Parties are organized. Gifts are wrapped and mailed. Holidays are orchestrated. Personal and business correspondence is maintained. But there is a difference!

Businesses feel justified in having sophisticated office equipment. They have hefty staplers, copying machines and filing systems. They hire receptionists to handle appointments, file clerks to file papers, secretaries to do the correspondence, accountants to keep track of money and project managers to organize major events. *Also, business managers do not vacuum their own floors, chauffeur the employees, fix the em-*

71

ployees' lunches, wash their clothes, read them stories, or give them hugs when the world looks grim. Need we say more? So what do we propose for the home manager?

Accept:

1. That you are running a small business.

2. That running a small business at home amidst the laundry is much harder than running it in a well-ordered office.

And then:

1. Set up your office as much like a business as possible. Set up a command center with a desk, supplies, phone and filing cabinet.

2. Buy office equipment and supplies to make the job easier.

3. Schedule time away from interruptions to run the office.

4. Set up systems that are simple, yet complete.

Systems used in the workplace are often the best source of ideas for the home office.

OFFICE HINTS

Sorting the Mail

Handle your mail at home as if you were in an office. The most important item to have on hand is a wastebasket for all the junk mail. Discard envelopes and flyers, then sort your mail. First, remove magazines and catalogs to be put in their designated areas, then remove mail that belongs to other members of the household. Then sort your mail into stacking plastic baskets with the following labels:

■ To Do—Things you must attend to in the short run.

■ Financial—Bills, bank statements, bank deposit and receipts, checks to be cashed.

■ Pending—Items that you will attend to later or are waiting for someone else to complete, ie., orders from catalogs, tickets and invitations.

■ To Read—Newsletters, brochures, handouts you want to read, but not pressing in the short run.

■ To File—All papers that you need to keep but which don't require action in the near future.

Rolodex

■ A Rolodex is the absolute best way to record addresses and phone numbers. It is a flexible and expandable system that doesn't require a whole day to set up or maintain. Each time an address changes, a new card is made and you move on. Keep stacks of cards near your telephone.

- Business cards can be trimmed and stapled onto Rolodex cards, or better yet, buy a Rolodex hole punch for business cards.

- "Yellow Pages" can be integrated into the cards by putting one category—such as "baby-sitters," "electricians" or "movie theaters"—on one card.

- Important numbers, such as the pediatrician's, can be found more easily if listed on another color card or put in plastic sleeves.

- Going to a restaurant? Write the number on a card when you call for reservations—leave the card out for the baby-sitter. Back in the Rolodex, it'll be handy for the next time you need to make reservations.

- Put the number of the pharmacist on the same card with your doctor so prescriptions can be called in easily.

- Put charge-card numbers on one card so that when ordering on the telephone, the number and expiration date is easily accessible.

Filing Hints

- There is a difference between filing something so you can find it again, and filing it into the archives of your life. At the end of each year, purge your files of everything you will not need during the upcoming year. You may need to refer to warranties but you will no doubt not need last year's phone bill. Place the preceding year's files in a banker's box near your present files for ready reference. Put them in the garage or basement the year after that.

- Make an income tax receipt file. Keep current year's receipts categorized in folders. If you do no other filing, you will love yourself for this one on April fifteenth.

- Make a calendar file. Use a clear vinyl sheet protector to hold invitations, announcements of business dinners and seminar information. Keep it in the front of your filing system. Mark your calendar with the date of the event, then put "CF" after it to indicate that the paperwork is in the calendar file.

- Use hanging files, with manila folders inside for sub-categorizing. Don't let your files get squeezed together too tightly.

Business Letterhead and Envelopes

- A business letterhead differs from personal stationery because it has a phone number on it. Have your stationery printed with your name, address and phone number at a quick print shop, and have it made into pads for easy storage and use. Have matching envelopes printed with just the return address so all family members can use them.

- Stationery, notepapers, envelopes and holiday cards can be stored in hanging file folders. The papers take up less space and are easy to retrieve. This hint works best for short stacks of paper.

- Have business cards printed up at a print shop. Include your name, address and phone number. Business cards save time when you want to give vital information to committee people, acquaintances and salespeople. And they are more impressive than bank deposit slips!

Speed Memos

- These are two-part carbon forms that allow you to keep a copy of your communications with others without having to use a copying machine. Businesses use them to save the cost and time of sending formal letters. Good to use when ordering items, delegating tasks that you want to follow up on and communicating with contractors. You'll have an exact record of what you asked people to do.

Accordion Folder Tickler System

- Have an accordion folder with 1–31 labels and place items under appropriate dates. Place birthday cards under date to be sent and airline tickets under date to be used, for example.

Dazzling Date Books

- The abundance of date books on the market is mind-boggling. Handsome leather and colorful plastic covers make date books tantalizing purchases. Date books often contain month/week/day-at-a-glance calendars and a notepad for jotting. Expanded versions have a section for addresses, goals and future projects. An excellent tool for the fragmented woman!

- At the very least, make a daily list of To Do's. Divide it into three parts: To Do At Home, To Do Out (errands) and To Call.

Computers in the Home

■ Take advantage of new technology to simplify home management. Use a computer to do home accounting, write checks, keep address lists, write letters and reports, do family schedules and much, much more. Connie's new Macintosh Plus allows her to design stationery in fifteen different type styles. She then copies her artistic creations on her personal copier on bright blue, yellow, green and orange papers.

Clear Vinyl Sheet Protectors

■ Clear vinyl sheet protectors are pockets with three holes for use in a binder. They hold 8 1/2-by-11-inch sheets of paper, or smaller. They come with a top or side opening. Terrific for use in notebooks to hold small pieces of paper, or in a filing system to hold small papers.

Credit-Card Collecting

■ The fewer credit cards you have the better. If you can get by with one major credit card, do so. You will have fewer to lose, to account for and to pay for.

■ If you must have several cards, keep track of them by Xeroxing all of them on an 8 1/2-by-11-inch sheet of paper. Then file the sheet with your other important papers.

Photos

- A date stamp (or line dater) is an excellent way to date photos developed without dates printed on them. Use a stamp pad with quick-drying ink or it will smear onto the next photo.

- A paper cutter is a terrific tool for cropping photos before putting them into an album. You'll get more pictures onto each page and keep only the important part of each photo. No more pages of chairs and tables with little tiny heads in one corner of the photo.

Managing Magazines

- Tear out important articles, put them into a "To Read" file and toss the bulky magazine. After reading, file the article under its subject, or better yet, toss it! Go to the library if you need to find an article on that subject again. Libraries have excellent filing and retrieval systems catered to full time by the staff. Let them do it.

Newspaper Articles

- A newspaper clipper near the area where you read the newspaper allows you to clip articles quickly and neatly.

- If you clip articles from the newspaper for future reference, use a copying machine that reduces the article to an 8 1/2-by-11-inch size. Copies are easier to put into files or notebooks, and they don't yellow and become difficult to read later on.

Key Location

■ Find a central place for stray keys. Pound tiny nails into the back of a cupboard door.

Return-Address Labels

■ Use labels anytime you are asked to fill out your name, address and phone. Carry labels in your purse or briefcase and keep a supply in your desk at home.

Letters

■ When you receive a letter, note on it items you want to include in your reply. Throw away the envelope if you have the address recorded.

Set Up a Home Office

9. Shopping Ahead

"We're out of milk! I'll run to the store to pick up a few things." An hour later, you are home with fifty dollars worth of groceries. The next day, you are out of peanut butter and off to the store again. Another fifty dollars is spent as you schlepp more items home. Time is wasted driving, parking and waiting in lines. Shopping is a perfect candidate for a planned simple system.

THE SIX-MONTH BULK-BUYING SYSTEM

Shop for Nonperishables Every Six Months.

- Nonperishables include paper products, toiletries, cleaning supplies, canned and bottled food, some dry foods, and drinks (assuming you can control how quickly they are consumed!) Make a list and continue to add to it over the six-month period. Then make one trip and buy in bulk. This will cost $400–500 and may not be possible for everyone.

Shop Monthly for Items that Keep for a Month in a Freezer.

- Examples include meat, bread, tortillas, butter, ice cream, cheese, frozen foods. Of course, it is easier with a full-sized freezer, but possible with a refrigerator freezer. Make a permanent list and continue to add to it.

Shop Weekly for Fruits, Vegetables and Dairy Products.

■ And this is a good time to pick up things you forgot in the monthly or six-month shopping. Make a permanent list and continue to add to it.

Provide Adequate Shelving for Bulk Buying.

■ Set your food storage area up like a mini grocery store so it is easy and pleasant to retrieve your food. Be sure to keep it separate from the opened food being used. Several opened jars of peanut butter can end your career as a six-month shopper.

Advantages of Six-Month Shopping Systems

■ You save time by not making a list each time you go to the store.

■ You carry the heavy cans, bottles and bulky paper products only twice a year. (You might even get help to do the six-month shopping!)

■ You never run out of the necessities.

■ You will spend less unscheduled time at the store.

Permanent Shopping Lists

- Make a permanent shopping list of everything you use in your house. Put the list in order according to the way things are arranged in your store, or make major headings: *Meat, Vegetables-Fruit, Bakery, Dry Goods, Paper Products, Canned Goods, Drinks, Toiletries, Cleaning Supplies*. Continue to improve your list by adding to it. Make a few copies at a time until you feel that you have a fairly complete list. Then make twenty copies and use as you need them.

- Make permanent lists for the health-food store, a big discount store you go to frequently, the office supply store.

- Permanent lists are just lists that were made once and kept. Not a difficult system to implement. Keep a folder for shopping lists in the kitchen.

Hang a "Things to Buy" Sheet on the Refrigerator.

- Let family members know that if an item is listed there, it will be bought on the next run to the grocery store. People will think of their needs in advance.

SHOPPING TIPS

Put Film Drop and Pickup on the Weekly Shopping List

- Have a drawer or basket where family members can leave film to be developed.

Greeting Cards

- Take your calendar of birthdays and other occasions to a card shop and buy cards for twelve months. Address the cards the same day. Fill in your name and message later.

- Buy greeting cards in advance for unexpected occasions. File by category: Humorous, Baby, Get Well, Thank-you, Congratulations. Cris sends informal thank you's on humorous prestamped postcards. Trés simple!

Give Consumable Gifts

- Help loved ones simplify by buying only consumable gifts: foodstuffs, flowers, toiletries. Find out what each person uses up!

Shopping Ahead

10. Food Planning

An overworked, frustrated woman said to us, "My kids will only eat hot dogs, turkey pies and scrambled eggs." And in the next breath, she said, "I feel terrible because I am not doing the pyllo dough and cute little shish kebabs for my family like my talented friends, but I can't do it all." She has her own solution staring at her. That's right! She can't do it all and, furthermore, she doesn't have to. She doesn't have people who want her to do it all. They want hot dogs. Great! That part of her life can be so simple. Why make things complicated that are screaming at you to be simple?

Freezing Foods

- Freeze soups and other liquids in loaf pans. When frozen, remove, wrap and stack in the freezer. No need to keep so many plastic containers around.

- Make spaghetti sauce in large batches and freeze. It gets better with time.

- On Sunday, make sandwiches for lunches for the week, and freeze in a bread bag. Kids can make up their own lunches by adding fruit, chips, and nuts without the mess of sandwich making.

- Freeze casseroles in single servings. Cuts down on overeating and allows one person to enjoy an interesting meal.

- Freeze meals in TV trays for someone who does not know how to cook but can use the oven or micro-wave.

- Batters can be kept frozen for up to two weeks for those who like fresh-baked muffins, cookies and breads.

- Whenever you make a dinner, make an extra one for the freezer.

Labeling Fridge Food

- Put a colored sticker on any food in the refrigera-tor that is being saved for a special occasion and should not be eaten by family or anyone else!

- Let people in the family label food they don't want others to eat. Helps prevent overeating to get one's fair share or hiding food in bedrooms. White cor-rection tape works well for this use.

Storing Foods

- Store unopened food such as cans, extra boxes of cereal, noodles and rice in a pantry area separate from opened food. You don't want an opened jar of peanut butter next to an unopened jar. Pretty soon, they are both opened.

Kids' Recipe Book

- Teach kids to cook by collecting recipes they can make by themselves in their own recipe book. Get them to make whole dinners as soon as they are able.

Meal Planning

- Plan meals for a week at a time. After three weeks, recycle your hard work by reusing the weekly menus again and again.

- Put each of your family's favorite meals on a three-by-five-inch index card. You probably will have no more than twenty. Pull seven cards per week and put in a new order!

- Designate certain nights of the week as Mexican Night, Soup Night, Pasta Night or Chicken Night. Then choose your favorite recipes.

Dinner Exchange

- Cook one night a week and deliver to three other families. They will deliver to you the other three nights. Great way to cover meals Monday through Thursday.

Food Planning

11. Organizing Children

Joel's teacher asked her fifth-grade class to write a short essay titled "Cleaning My Room." Joel wrote, "I like to clean my room for two reasons. I hardly have any toys to put away. For instance, I only have eleven toys. It only takes me three minutes to clean my room. I only have one shelf." Kids don't need tons of toys in their rooms. Store the possessions your child is ambivalent about in a lidded box in the garage, or on a high shelf. Recycle unwanted toys monthly. Children enjoy being surrounded by current favorites and can be taught to simplify!

Tips for Toys and Games

■ Store kids' toys, games, books, puzzles and projects in a toy library (storage cabinet). Then, periodically, "check out" the things they want to play with at the moment. The visual bombardment of too much dulls kids' interest in their toys.

■ Start a Grandfather's Chest for each child in which to keep favorite toys, clothes, stuffed animals, projects, badges and other important memorabilia that cannot be put into photo albums. This keeps all the things to save for each child in one place and not in several different boxes in the garage.

■ Set aside a box where miscellaneous pieces can be tossed, then matched up with incomplete toys or games. Store it out of the children's room so other things will not be added.

- Put toys with small pieces into drawstring bags or large, freezer-size Ziploc bags. Label the bags and toss out the boxes the toys came in. Clear plastic refrigerator containers, sweater boxes and mini laundry baskets can also be labeled and used.

Clutter Baskets

- A basket or area to "dump" kids' things throughout the day can keep active clutter to a manageable level. Then, every evening after dinner, the kids can empty it and put away their belongings.

- A mini laundry basket or dishpan is an excellent storage place for little shoes.

Coding Kids

- Color code your kids. Let each have hangers, toothbrush, laundry basket, toy baskets in his/her own color. Why? So you can easily sort laundry, find toothbrushes, bathroom glasses, etc.

- When you have kids whose clothes are close in size or style, code them by putting "1" on the oldest child's clothes and "11" on the next child's clothes. Then, when you hand the clothes down, you need only add a 1 to the piece of clothing. The second child will always think he wears size 11!

School Papers and Art

- If you keep ten things a year for one child for sixteen years, you will have saved 160 items. Multiply that by the number of children you have. Simplify, simplify!

- When a child brings home a large art project or builds a model that cannot be kept forever, take a photo of the child with the creation. You can even blow it up to hang on the wall.

- Clear contact paper preserves messy and beautiful works of art for preschoolers.

- Keep in a convenient place a large plastic sweater box or file box in which to toss school papers and projects that are not ready for either the trash or a keepsake box. Each month, have your child toss out the papers that he doesn't want. Put the rest in a keepsake box. Be sure to date everything. (An artist's portfolio works well for preschoolers' artwork.)

The Limbo Box

- Junk in kids' rooms? You think it is junk, they think it is treasure. Give them a Limbo Box. Kids, especially teenagers, get to store things they are unprepared to throw away and are no longer using. The Limbo Box can be put on a top closet shelf or stored in the garage.

Storage by the Door

- Each child needs his own place to put papers, books and belongings taken back and forth to school and activities. If these things are always dropped near the door, it makes sense to store them near the door.

  Young children: A basket to corral stray toys, school artwork, a jacket or boots.

School children: A hook for a backpack; a letter tray or basket for school papers, magazines, library books, Brownies' handbook.

High Schoolers: A letter tray or bulletin board for messages and permission slips. They can keep the rest of their belongings in their rooms.

Library Books

- Remove cards from library books as soon as you get home from the library. Put them in a safe place. When it's time to return the books, match up the cards with the books and you won't forget to return them.

Rolodex Cards

- Let children have their own color-coded Rolodex cards for friends' numbers in your main family Rolodex.

Family Calendar

- If you keep a central wall calendar for the family, color code activities for family members—red for Johnny, blue for mom, green for dad.

Emergency Phone Numbers

- As soon as children have phones in their rooms, they need their own list of emergency numbers.

Calendars for Children

■ Give children a calendar for listing their activities as soon as they can read. It prepares them for using a pocket calendar when they reach junior high school and need to record assignments.

Organizing Children

12. Tips for Trips

I hoped that the trip would be the best of all journeys: a journey into ourselves.

—Shirley MacLaine

Traveling allows you to see the world from a fresh perspective. Unfortunately, preparing for a trip is often so stressful that the benefits are hard to discern. Here are some hints to ease the burden.

Packing Toiletries

- Keep a toiletries kit packed and ready to go; fill it with shampoo, extra razor, extra deodorant, etc. It is easier on the traveler and easier on the person left at home if the shampoo is not removed from the shower.

- Use half-empty containers of cosmetics for travel toiletries, replacing them with whole containers for home use.

- Keep a separate toiletries kit packed for children, including a night-light, baby aspirin and other items needed specifically for children when traveling.

Ditty Bags

- A ready-to-go ditty bag for each child, with toothbrush, toothpaste, hairbrush, lip balm, and whatever else they use, can be kept for short jaunts, overnighters, camping trips and family trips.

Travel Notebooks and Lists

- Any time you make a travel list, keep the list and improve on it the next time you travel. Shortly, you will have a fairly foolproof list to help you maximize the pleasure of traveling and minimize the stress.

- A travel file or notebook filled with permanent lists can make getting out of town simple. Lists can include: packing lists for each member of the family, things to do before leaving town, a permanent camp list, a permanent ski list.

- A travel notebook to leave with the baby-sitter or house-sitter can include the following household information: a household maintenance list, location of water shutoff, phone numbers of repair people, watering schedule, names of neighbors, use of appliances.

- Traveling without children can be relaxing, but the preparation can be tedious. Put the following information in a notebook and update the information each time you go out of town: Baby-sitter information list; doctors' names and phone numbers; emergency numbers; locations of schools; map showing schools, doctors' offices, church, play-

93

grounds, pool, friends' homes; medical permission slip; children's friends' names, addresses and phone numbers; parents' and grandparents' work and home phone numbers; children's schedules.

Emergency Car Kit

■ Keep emergency car supplies in an army-surplus canvas bag or a ripstop nylon bag. Pack a blanket, flares, flashlight, jumper cables, tools, jack, oil and ice scraper.

Packing Tips

■ Clothes can be folded, rolled or stuffed. Every fold is a potential crease. Clothes should be folded so any sharp creases that may appear emphasize the structural lines of the garment.

■ Not every garment that can be rolled should be. Rolling is mainly an alternative for casual clothes —nightwear, underwear, accessories and wrinkle-free synthetics. Roll some clothes that will be worn together in sets.

■ Stuffing some things into others in your suitcase saves space. Shoes can be stuffed with rolled socks or a secret bag of jewelry.

■ Put name, address and phone number inside the suitcase.

Wrinkle-proof Traveling

■ Arriving at your destination unruffled, unwrinkled, and uncrushed is an art. Below are six ways to avoid wrinkles and preserve creases:

1. Distribute the weight in your suitcase evenly.

2. Pack tightly, but not too tightly.

3. Pack when you are alone. You do better without distractions.

4. Avoid damaging juxtaposition of colors and hardware.

5. Cushion fragile fabrics with tissue paper, dry-cleaner bags, or super-soft clothing.

6. Fold and roll clothes properly. Read Cris Evatt's *How to Pack Your Suitcase and Other Travel Tips* (New York: Fawcett, 1987) for complete instructions.

13. It's O.K. to Delegate

The sage does nothing, but nothing is left undone.

—Lao-Tzu

Delegation is the final reward of simplifying and systematizing. First you simplify, then organize. Once you do these two steps, delegation is quite natural. Think of the total job of home management as a giant checkerboard with each task represented by a square. The object of the game is to give away all of the jobs you do not like, are not good at or that someone else can do to your satisfaction. The more defined the job, the more possible it is to give away. And, of course, the simpler the job, the more likely you are to find a competent person to do it.

DELEGATOPHOBIA

Is delegating hard for you? Do you have a subconscious list of excuses that keeps you from assigning tasks to others. Let's look at common excuses we all use to avoid delegating. While you read the excuses, keep in mind that delegating extends the results of what one person can *do*, to what one person can *manage*. Delegating promotes you from worker to manager.

"I don't feel right about delegating."

Will others love you more, less or just the same if someone else gets the job done? And how will you feel? These basic questions must be answered before you can feel good about delegating. Remember, we are not talking about delegating the job of parenting or being a loving spouse; we are talking about sewing on buttons, cleaning dishes, returning videos and picking up hooks for the closet.

"I can't afford to pay others."

Yes, it costs money to hire others. And the more professional people are, the higher their wages. What is your time worth? If a day of life is worth five hundred dollars, wouldn't it make sense to hire someone for fifty dollars to do a dreaded job?

"It's easier to do it myself."

Family members and coworkers are not out to get you, but as humans, they have clever tactics for avoiding work. Some whine, "Do I have to?"; others say, "Yes, I'll do it," and then forget. Getting out of work is an art for many people. Persistence, in the long run, will earn you the title of "Manager." Give in to others, and you'll find yourself moaning resentfully, "It's easier to do it myself." In the short run, perhaps it is!

"I don't have time to organize the job."

If you take the time to set up a job for someone else, you will eventually have more time. It takes time to make time. Spend a couple of hours preparing jobs to be delegated while you are vacationing—away from children, work pressures and daily commitments. Or skip a luncheon, dinner or meeting and use the time to set up jobs. There is always time if you are willing to give up some current busyness.

"Nobody does it right."

The goal for you and the delegatee is to be successful. In order for the delegatee to hold up his/her end of the deal, you must describe the task completely, train the person as needed and supply the proper tools. You must communicate your standards to your assistant. Communication is the key. Don't leave people guessing.

DELEGATING HINTS

Delegatees.

- You can delegate to a spouse and children. There are people for hire. Professionals charge a hefty sum, but can be expected to be well trained—if you choose them well. Also, teenagers and college students can be hired. True, their schedules are hectic, but they charge less. For fifteen dollars, you can hire a teenager to help you clean out the garage for four hours. Your husband will be thrilled.

Delegate Jobs to Yourself.

- When you delegate to others, you organize the job and set a time limit. Prepare your own tasks as if you were giving them to someone else. It's lack of preparation and interrupted time that makes a job difficult. Treat yourself as well as you treat the people you pay, and you may find doing the job a pleasure.

Use a Timer

■ Set a timer for sixty minutes, then "go for it" on some big task like cleaning the basement or a cluttered closet. Then quit and start again the next day.

■ While working and studying at home, it is hard to ignore household tasks. Set a timer for fifty minutes of study then ten minutes of doing quick tasks—folding the laundry, making an easy casserole, tidying a room.

Delegating Child Care

One of the most common sources of guilt in women is mothers' delegation of child care tasks to others. The most comforting counsel we can provide is this: Mothering is a great deal more than the myriad tasks involved in caring for a child. Delegating some—even many—of these tasks does not mean you are delegating your role as mother. Relax and take care of yourself and your child or children by delegating as many tasks as is reasonable for you.

Do We Need a Baby-sitter Tonight?

■ Getting baby-sitters when there are special events can be a complicated task. Make a chart with columns for Event, Date, Times, Baby-sitter Hired, Phone Number. Post it next to the phone.

■ The time from 5:00 P.M. until 7:00 P.M. is always hectic with small children! Hire a sitter for this time—transition time—and relax with your husband while the children are entertained by another.

Fabulous Forms and Checklists

- Forms and checklists capture information so that you do not always have to return to "point zero." Businesses use forms in abundance. We believe home managers can become more organized by using forms and checklists. On the pages following are examples from Connie's *Home Management Systems Notebook*:

    Household Instructions Form. Can be copied and used for any home. An essential form for a house-sitter, baby-sitter, or a guest who is in your home when you are not.

    Baby-sitter Information Sheet. A must when leaving your children with a sitter. You'll need several copies.

    Baby-sitter Instructions Sheet. Lets the baby-sitter know your rules so things will be done as you like them to be while you are gone.

    Consent for Emergency Treatment Form. Allows your baby-sitter to authorize medical care in your absence. Weekly Home Maintenance. Gives guidelines for essential weekly chores. Add or subtract for your own priorities.

    Weekly and Periodic Home Maintenance
    These are Connie's essential weekly and periodic chores: you'll probably have your own priorities. Use our list as a model for making your own.

- Forms can be handwritten, typewritten or computer printouts. They can have pictures and be printed on colored paper. Be imaginative!

Household Instructions

Extra House Key	
Electrical Breaker Box	
Water Cutoff	
Thermostat	
Alarm System Box	
Neighbor	Phone
Other	
Alarm Company	Phone
Veterinarian	Phone
Electrician	Phone
Plumber	Phone
Air Conditioning/Heating Co.	Phone
Appliance Repair	Phone
Garbage Pickup	
Newspapers	
Yard Care	
Animals	
School	
Child's Name	
Address	Phone
School	
Child's Name	
Address	Phone
School	
Child's Name	
Address	Phone

Baby-sitter Information

You Are at the Home of	
Address	
The Phone Number Here Is	
Our Home Is Located	
Father's Work Number	
Mother's Work Number	
Neighbor	Phone
Address	
Location	
Relative/Friend	Phone
All Emergency	
Police	
Fire	
Poison Control	
Children's Doctor	Phone
Address	
Hospital Name	Phone
Address	
Dentist	Phone
Address	
Insurance Co. Policy No.	
Special Allergy or Other Instructions	

Baby-sitter Instructions

You Are at the Home of
Name
Address   Cross Street
Phone
We are going
Phone   Est. time of return

FIRE
Leave house immediately with all of the children in hand. Phone fire department AFTER YOU REACH A NEIGHBOR'S HOUSE.

Emergency 911

Police District #_____

Fire Department _____

DON'T OPEN THE DOOR TO ANYONE unless we have told you specifically who might drop by. You may have visitors only after asking us. If you do have a visitor, it is understood that the family room and kitchen will be cleaned up.

NEVER LEAVE CHILDREN ALONE IN THE BATHTUB. Get the towels, toys, cloths and diapers together in the bathroom before children get into the bath.

PLEASE LIMIT PHONE CALLS TO 10 MINUTES. There might be an emergency, and we might have to reach you.

LIMIT CHILDREN'S TV TO SPECIAL PROGRAMS. Watch allowed programs with the children. Otherwise, put off your own TV watching until the children are in bed.

CLEAN UP THE KITCHEN, FAMILY ROOM AND CHIL-DREN'S ROOMS BEFORE WE GET HOME.

Consent for Emergency Treatment and/or Surgery

We, the undersigned, hereby authorize

to consent to medical treatment and/or surgery for our minor child(ren)

CHILD'S NAME	DATE OF BIRTH
CHILD'S NAME	DATE OF BIRTH
CHILD'S NAME	DATE OF BIRTH

effective from
to

Signature of Parents/Guardian

Date

Weekly Home Maintenance

GENERAL
Carpets—vacuum, including stairs
Hardwood floors—wash with water
Windowsills—wipe clean
Baseboards—dust
Wastebaskets—empty
Furniture—dust
Glass tables—polish
Mini blinds—dust

KITCHEN
Kitchen grill—(when used) clean (no abrasives)
Stove, countertops, sink, refrigerator top & sides, small
    appliances—clean & polish.
Microwave interior—clean (no abrasives)

LIVING ROOM/TV ROOM/DINING ROOM
Fireplace glass doors—clean both sides
Hearth—damp mop
Mantle—wipe clean

BATHS
Floor—wash with cleaning solvent
Tub, sink, toilet—scrub & polish
Mirror—polish
Towels—straighten

BEDROOMS
Beds—change sheets, square corners; side & top even

BASEMENT (PLAYROOM)
Carpet—vacuum

BASEMENT (LAUNDRY)
Appliances, folding table—wipe clean (move items on top)

FRONT PORCH (OUTSIDE)
Floor—sweep

Periodic Home Maintenance

GENERAL
Oak woodwork — oil
Brass doorknobs & heater grates — polish
Wood furniture — oil

KITCHEN
Refrigerator interior — clean (no abrasives)
Cupboard under sink — wipe clean

LIVING ROOM/TV ROOM/DINING ROOM
Bookshelves — remove contents and clean
Brass bucket — shine

BATHS
Tile — scrub
Medicine chest interior — remove contents and clean

BEDROOMS
Closet shelves — remove contents and clean
Mattress — turn
Bookshelves — remove contents and clean

BASEMENT
Toy shelves, tables, bookshelves
Couches, chairs, furniture — remove contents and clean
Stair railing & side of stairs — wipe clean

BASEMENT (LAUNDRY ROOM)
Floor — sweep & damp mop
Shelves — wipe clean

FRONT PORCH OR DECK (OUTSIDE)
Floor — damp mop with solvent
Windowsills & door — wipe clean

GARAGE
Floor — sweep

OUR HOME TASKS

	MOM	DAD		STONEY	CASEY	SITTER		HOUSE CLEANER
MON	Pack lunches	Casey to School		Feed dog	Clean room			Laundry Floors
	carpool			Soccer	ballet	Dinners		
TUES	groceries	Dry cleaning		Feed dog				Iron

It's O.K. to Delegate

107

14. Responsible Kids

It is my belief that no one (except infants and individuals who are ill or physically disabled) should have a free ride when it comes to the work of the house. This does not mean that everyone should share equally; circumstances may dictate otherwise. But neither does it mean that one person should become the sacrificial household lamb.

— Marjorie Hansen Shaevitz
  The Superwoman Syndrome

Too often women become the slaves of the household, while children get by without contributing. Women today are busier than ever and cannot let this happen.

The best thing we can do for our children is train them to do all of the jobs listed on the Home Manager Job Description in chapter 1. Children are taken to judo, ballet, art, modeling and self-improvement classes of all kinds. Hours are spent carpooling, rooting at their games and watching their performances. Some parents spend thousands of dollars a year on private schools and many hours doing volunteer work in the classroom and for the P.T.A. Other people have been given the major role of teaching our children other skills, but there is *no one* teaching our children to be home managers except us.

If we do not teach our children to be home managers, they will operate with a tremendous handicap when they leave home. Do we want our daughter to marry the first man she meets because she doesn't know how to handle money or mow the lawn? Do we want our son to choose a woman because she will wash and iron his clothes?

Even if you have full-time help, consider giving your children the *opportunity* to learn household skills. Even if you do not need your child's help, make sure he/she does every job on the job description before he/she leaves home. Children must learn to do maintenance tasks so they can be more successful and effective in the world.

CHILDREN AS HEDONISTS

Unfortunately, most children don't care that doing chores will help them in adult life. They just want to play—focus their attention on Go-Bots, TransFormers, and Barbie dolls. Because most children are incredibly hedonistic, they invent dozens of chore-evasion schemes which you need to recognize before delegating. Here are some of them:

■ **Children Forget Chores.** How can kids do chores if they forget what needs to be done? (They have fabulous memories for their own wants and needs.)

■ **Children Do Chores Slowly.** A great way to frustrate a parent who wants a job done *now*.

- **Children Leave Chores Incomplete.** Their minds drift, so the job doesn't get done. Some kids brag after a task is three quarters finished, "Look at the great job I did, Dad!"

- **Children Make Noise While Working.** They stomp their feet, yell, curse and act obnoxious. Parents dislike noise, and kids know it.

- **Children Shift Blame.** "It's his turn to do the dishes, not mine. Why do you always pick on me?"

- **Children Fake Incompetence.** Kids do their tasks poorly so a parent will think, "Next time I'll do the job myself. It's so much easier than dealing with kids." Who needs this headache?

- **Children Charm.** When asked to do a job, children bat their lashes, and parents sigh, "Isn't he cute. Looks just like me. How can I ask him to do those chores? He's only twelve."

- **Children Make Excuses.** Kids have a repertoire of creative reasons for not doing work. "I don't have time;" or "I've done enough work today. You're being unfair." "I'd love to mom, but . . ."

- **Children Intimidate.** Kids scowl. Parents cower. Some parents even fear their three-year-olds.

- **Children Procrastinate.** They wait until the last minute to do their chores and drive you nuts wondering if they will get done on time.

WHAT ABOUT CONSEQUENCES?

Reminding children to do chores is frustrating. Each time a parent reminds a child to do a chore, the child feels nagged and the parent feels like a drill sergeant. We have discovered that a system of "chores and consequences" lightens up this heavy drama.

Consequences are necessary for some children all of the time and all children, some of the time. When our friend Joan posted her ten-year-old stepson Larry's list of daily chores, she added consequences to the bottom of his Chorechart because Larry forgets to do his chores unless he is reminded ad nauseam. Many kids are self-absorbed and need consequences for motivation.

A consequence is a penalty for misbehavior. Consequences do not have to be severe, but they can be if the misdemeanor warrants it. Creating consequences is an art. The more you know about them, the more respect you will have from your children.

How do you know if you need to know more about consequences? It's easy to find out. Does what you tell your children "go in one ear and out the other"? Do your children do what you say when you say it—or after you've said it until you are livid? People whose children act deaf need to know about the fine art of doling out penalties.

KINDS OF CONSEQUENCES

We discovered three kinds of consequences. "Natural consequences" happen to your child when he/she disobeys and you do nothing; but the world slaps him/her on the wrist. For example, if little Lisa does not do her homework, her teacher (the world) has her write five hundred lines of "I will do my homework on time." She misses five recesses and suffers the natural consequences of her forgetfulness.

Then there are "related consequences." You come up with a penalty that reflects the nature of the crime. If Jeffrey isn't in bed by nine, then the next night he must be in bed by eight. The consequences and the misdeed are related.

Lastly, there are "unrelated consequences." You create a penalty that is absurd, totally unrelated to the offense. You do this for shock value. Unrelated consequences have to be carefully thought up ahead of time. The purpose is to wake the child up, make him/her notice you and your intention to have chores done on time.

When you create consequences for your child, be imaginative. Common consequences can include no TV, earlier bedtime, no dessert, being grounded, demerits and additional chores. Find out what works with your child. What may entice one child to do his chores on time may cause another child to say "So what!"

HELPFUL HINTS

Posting Daily Chores

- Post chores on bulletin boards, refrigerators or walls.

- List chores on brightly colored paper and place in a clear Plexiglas frame to make the list look official.

- Post chore lists at eye level.

- Include times and consequences on Chorecharts. (See Joel's chart on page 116).

Rewarding Children for Jobs Well Done

- Praising children for good work lets them know how they are doing. And it makes them feel good.

- Reward with colorful stickers, a special dessert, some time with you, or a financial bonus. Most of the time a smile and a hug should be enough.

- Keep in mind that children want to please *and* they could care less. Their feelings are inconsistent because humans are inconsistent. Reinforce helpful behaviors. Rewards are a way to do this.

Have Family Meetings

- At a family meeting, go over the Home Manager's Job Description to find out who can do what jobs. Also poll the family to find out what is important to each person, and what is not. You may discover that paper plates work best for dishes. You may find that everyone likes to fold clothes in front of their favorite TV show.

Don't Tamper with Their Allowance

- Dr. Haim G. Ginott claims, "An allowance is not a reward for good behavior nor a punishment for chores not done. It is an educational device that has a distinct purpose: to provide experience in the use of money by exercising choices and assuming responsibilities."

Billy's Schedule

MORNING
- Brush Teeth ☐
- Make Bed ☐
- Get Dressed ☐
- Clean Up Room ☐
- Eat Breakfast ☐
- Take Out Trash ☐

TAKE TO SCHOOL
- Helmet ☐
- Backpack ☐
- Lunch ☐
- Spelling Words ☐
- Library Books ☐

AFTER SCHOOL
- Set Table ☐
- Do Homework—One Hour ☐

AFTER DINNER
- Clear Table ☐
- Bath ☐
- Clothes in Hamper ☐
- Floss & Brush Teeth ☐

Joel's Chorechart

TIME	To Be Done By: 8:00 a.m.	To Be Done By: 9:00 p.m.	
SUNDAY	TRASH	TOYS LAUNDRY	SPELLING FLOSS
MONDAY	TRASH LUNCH	TOYS LAUNDRY	BATH READING FLOSS
TUESDAY	TRASH LUNCH	TOYS LAUNDRY	READING FLOSS
WEDNESDAY	TRASH LUNCH	TOYS LAUNDRY	BATH READING FLOSS
THURSDAY	TRASH LUNCH	TOYS LAUNDRY	READING FLOSS
FRIDAY	TRASH LUNCH	TOYS LAUNDRY	BATH FLOSS
SATURDAY	BY NOON: CHANGE BED NEATEN ROOM	TRASH LAUNDRY	TOYS FLOSS

Consequences
1. Jobs not done by 8:00 a.m. equal 8:00 p.m. bedtime that night.
2. Jobs not done by 9:00 a.m. equal 8:00 p.m. bedtime the next night.
3. Reading makeup: ½ hour missed equals 1 hour makeup on Saturday or Sunday.
4. Homework: Forgotten to bring home or turn in equals 8:00 p.m. bedtime same night.

_____ Chorechart

TIME	To Be Done By:	To Be Done By:
SUNDAY		
MONDAY		
TUESDAY		
WEDNESDAY		
THURSDAY		
FRIDAY		
SATURDAY		
Consequences		

15. Uncomplicate Life

Simplify every day in every way! First, eliminate the unimportant, whether it be relationships, responsibilities, possessions or self-concepts. Once you have done that, *organize* so that repetitive tasks become easy systems and do not require valuable creative energy. And last, *delegate* or give away tasks that others can do acceptably.

You will need daily encouragement and inspiration to begin simplifying, so we are concluding with quotes that can be made into affirmations. Put your favorites on index cards and post on a wall. When you read the quotes, remember that successful living is a journey toward simplicity and a triumph over confusion. Good luck on your journey!

I have learned by some experience, by many examples, and by the writings of countless others before me, also occupied in the search, that certain environments, certain modes of life, certain rules of conduct are more conducive to inner and outer harmony than others. There are, in fact, certain roads that one may follow. Simplification is one of them.

—Anne Morrow Lindbergh

The simple life retains its relevance even in the midst of renewed prosperity and the much ballyhooed appeal of the Yuppie way of life. Liberating oneself from the addiction of consumerism and careerism promotes inner peace.

—David E. Shi

Have nothing in your houses that you do not know to be useful, or believe to be beautiful.

—William Morris

It is positively rare, but tremendously exhilarating, to find a woman, as one does now and then, who is courageous enough to furnish her home with an eye single to comfort and practical utility, and who refuses to have her home leveled to a plane of mediocrity by filling it with useless bric-a-brac and gimcracks, the only mission of which seems to be to offend the eye and accumulate dust.

—Edward Bok

It's the little things that drive you crazy—the broken heel, the stain, the drip. If you take care of the little things, the big things become manageable.

—Heloise

All that is contrary to the essential must be relinquished.

—Emile Durkheim

For my part, as I grow older, I am more and more inclined to reduce my baggage, to lop off superfluities. I become more and more in love with simple things and simple folk—a small house, a hut in the woods, a tent on the shore. The show and splendor of great houses, elaborate furnishings, stately halls, oppress me, impose upon me.

—John Burroughs

There is more to life than increasing its speed. The outward behavior of a man is at once the sign and proof of the inner state.

—Anonymous

Let every moment carry away all that it brought.

—Andre Gide

Great simplicity is only won by an intense moment or by years of intelligent efforts or both. It represents one of the most arduous conquests of the human spirit—the triumph of feeling and thought over the natural sins of language.

—T.S. Eliot

One day, observing a child drinking water out of his hands, Diogenes cast away a cup from his pouch with the words: "A child has beaten me in plainness of living." He also threw away his bowl when in like manner he saw a child who had broken his plate taking up lentils with the hollow part of a morsel of bread.

—Laertius

If you wish to make Pythocles rich, do not add to his money, but subtract from his desires.

—Epicurus

Live simply, so that others may simply live.

—Gandhi

All the big people are simple, as simple as the unexplored wilderness. They love the universal things that are free to everybody. Light and air and food and love and some work are enough. In the varying phases of these cheap and common things, the great lives have found their joy.

—Carl Sandburg

In the beginner's mind, there are many possibilities. In the expert's, there are few.

—Suzuki Roshi

I am strongly drawn to the simple life and am often oppressed by the feeling that I am engrossing an unnecessary amount of the labour of my fellow men. I regard class differences as contrary to justice and, in the last resort, based on force. I also consider that plain living is good for everybody, physically and mentally.

—Albert Einstein

Unless a man is simple, he cannot recognize God, the Simple One.

—Bengali saying

Contributors

We would like to thank the following women for contributing organizing hints to this book.

Alice Applebaum; Denver, CO
Marilyn Brenengen; Englewood, CO
Risa Buckstein; Denver, CO
Elizabeth Ellis; Littleton, CO
Kristine Erving; Palo Alto, CA
Sally Freelen; Stanford, CA
Barbara Glacel; Burke, VA
Linda Houston; Denver, CO
Martha Campbell Iler; Englewood, CO
Bonnie Kailey; Westminster, CO
Loretta Keim; Anchorage, AK
Sally Kurtzman; Denver, CO
Becky Perry; Englewood, CO
Dotty Putnam; Lafayette, CO
Kathy Schmidt; Palo Alto, CA
Evelyn Smith; Colorado Springs, CO
Marilyn Spangenberg; Denver, CO
Marcia Strickland; Denver, CO
Gayle Weeks; Napa, CA

To Our Readers

We welcome tips and ideas for simplifying and organizing your life!

Our address is:

**Simply Organized
P.O. Box 788
Menlo Park, CA 94026**